EVERYTHING
LINCOLNBYRD
VOLUME 1

outskirtspress
DENVER, COLORADO

Table of Contents

Atlanta, Georgia

1 | Life

The personality of this generation has been fueled by a beautiful archetype, of what life should represent. The dream was sold and bought by many; even me. So I express no regret that no one caught on before it was too late.

The "Danger Ahead; Proceed with Caution" signs have always been present, or did we choose to ignore them?

Relationships are doomed from the beginning. The vision of a healthy, and happy relationship is a mirror image, of what is portrayed in the most popular videos, songs, and TV shows, or even your upbringing.

This sets the state of mind of a perfect relationship, and this is the lie; and what causes it to fail.

How can you love someone who you don't even know... someone who doesn't know you, or someone who don't even know themselves?"

The emotional is the matrix, and the physical is the reality, while the flesh keeps us weak. The mind and the heart keeps you grounded, and prayer is always a way to fight back.

It's the awareness of one's self and purpose, and that's where the love comes in. Only then is it at its purest form, and without doubt or reservation does it truly work. This is the kind of love a small child possesses.

A love that is not tainted with this world, and corrupt in the lie. A love that is dependent on you for their every need, and you give it willingly. A seed you nourish, and feed, and pray it grows.

And that's where it ends.

I live in Atlanta Georgia, and I work at a major metropolitan hospital, that is located in Midtown. I'm also a rouge mixologist, and I do volunteer work at a homeless shelter.

But most important I am an American author, and writing people's stories is my passion.

I have bartended at some of the most popular clubs in Atlanta, and for the underground elite. Tending bar is an excellent way of getting ideas, and information to write, and so is working with the homeless. People want to tell their story, and have someone to listen without judgement.

Atlanta is a melting pot of everything. When I say everything, I mean everything! Whatever your mind can conceive, can and does exist, for the good and the bad. Once again I make no apologies: this is our world, and this is our time.

I have encountered the weird, the evil, and the good. Not by choice, but by living and taking chances, and being a component of this ever changing world. I'm no license psychologist, relationship guide, or expert on love.

I'm your average guy, who has been asked by too many of his peers. To take time out of writing other things and write a book about our time, life, love and relationship's right now.

You can't earn a degree in this; because the game is always changing. Society can't educate enough professors to keep up.

Only the players stay the same and the books are always sold out.

2 | Searching For That One

I have received about all the advice from friends and my mother. I have entertained the motivational ideas, and game changing remedies. I have examined all the self-love books, Oprah, House wives of anything, and radio seem to ride on.

The things that hold our imagination is evident of the social conscience that is feeding these venues. This is what contributes to the mindset that has changed the game forever, and what exist in this new way of thinking.

The things I write are blunt and true. It has taken me years to really learn how to listen to what a person is really trying to tell me. Some people are desperate, and are really asking for help. I've learned to be "Quick to listen, and Slow to speak," and then I write it.

I've kept a journal of the conversations I would have, during happy hour, or who ever needed to say what's on their mind. Mostly because I wanted it to be relevant to things that are going on in our time, and I titled it

"Everything."

My stories reveal what's really on people's minds.

They also share dark secrets about the underbelly of this world, and the evil that men do. My journals are about men and women sharing their life's heartaches over loud music, Apple martinis, and Hennessey.

I even had one lady sit at my bar, and tell me that her marriage would be perfect, if she could just get her husband's mother out of their life. She said things would be like they were when they first met; if the mother would just mind her own business.

"Why don't you and your husband have a sit- down with her?" I asked.

She looked at me with glazed eyes, and a hazy mist that surrounded her green contacts. She took a long sip of her drink and said. "Then me and my kids would have nowhere to live, and I wouldn't have a babysitter." I looked into her desperate eyes and I moved on to the next customer.

"You cannot have it both ways nothing is free, not even grandmothers."

Wisdom is patience, it is also the way to success at whatever endeavor that happens to be your thing. And most importantly you have to have a purpose for yourself, not for your mate or your kids. Solitude begins with self-first. Then you share what you have learned. Then your joy and wisdom can be passed on.

3

Dating

The traditional dating scene of the "Good ole days are gone." After years of living in a city like Atlanta, and a few others, I have come to realize that in our time they all have something in common.

The sexes are confused, and nothing is sacred. I ran across a few popular dating sites, and yea, I have been curious. I felt maybe I was missing out on something. I would see the commercials of all those couples who had found love, and they looked so happy.

I'm not keeping up with the Browns. But when it came time to choose what type of relationship I was looking for. I never knew I had so many dating options to choose from.

Men seeking women

Men seeking Men

Women seeking married men

Women seeking women

Women seeking sugar daddy's and so on.

I was truly confused, all I wanted was someone to talk to, and maybe some hot 'butt naked' sex every now and then, without all that baggage.

What happened to all the girls of my past? I guess they live in an alternate reality called Facebook, Twitter, and Instagram.

The reason those things never appealed to me is because I don't have enough time or patience to post my day to day activities; besides who would care?

The older I get the more I realize I'm old fashion when it comes to relationships, or maybe I'm insecure. But don't get it twisted when I say insecure. I don't mean my manhood, but my financial status. Besides that: I have more heart than most.

A stable household, relationship, or even a friendship, begins with some type of trust. People say "I don't trust no one". That's a lie you have to trust someone, somewhere, at least seven times a day.

You trust pain, because you know when it comes around, and why it's here. Two things will happen either it will make you or break you. Actually pain is a growing mechanism, it will teach you to appreciate life, and to not go back to what caused that pain. Learn to love the ones who truly love you.

I probably wouldn't like a run way model or a highly successful woman, but I would fall for a Rosario Dawson. Because I believe she is modestly extravagant, and I believe excitement is made by the willing participants.

I could own a plain townhouse that's immaculate on the inside, with a four door Altima and still be happy. But would my lady be happy? And that's where the problem lies.

4 | Self-Awareness

No one can live in this world, and not be a part of it. I have to love and respect our earth because it was made by God. I cannot fall into the hopes and dreams of others because then I would neglect mine, and his plan for me.

Some people look at my view of our world, like I have less faith. So I must play it cool, I call it Luciano cool. I have to trust my own instincts, and discipline my own demons.

Only I know the medium in which my demons can exist, and what feeds them. Awareness of who and what we truly are, is the awakening that was prophesized to come. It's the maturity of our faith, love, and the realization that we are human, and we will make mistakes.

I never judge anyone, but I know that people have their own motives, or what makes them tick. In our own way, we all strive for a higher understanding, and we all have our own journey to travel.

So I judge no one, but I embrace the idea that we all are seeking a truth. Amen.

I have developed a level of existence, that I know exist in nature, and I call it "The middle ground."

Energy has many levels but it has one that is constant, a medium, or middle that can coexist with another. Yes, life has its highs and its lows. In order for it to stay in motion it has to have an even balance, or it can get distracted. I view relationships in the same way.

Let me explain.

The middle is the neutral ground, which I mean mentally and spiritually.

No matter what happens in your life, good or bad, we are grounded on one energy plain. Whether it be religion, prayer, family, drugs, or the children, there is always something constant, and when there's not we have a problem.

The problem is the interference that is going to deter you from your journey on this earth. We all know the procrastinations we possess that lead to our failures in life.

Relationships work the same way, if you and your significant other can find a neutral point. Where, what you could call an agreement, or harmony is established. It means you have established a common ground. A place where everyone has the same interest.

If you work together this is your reality, love it or hate it. Whatever it is that you and your mate agree on, is your sacred ground. Whether it be the kids, sex, money, religion, or even love.

This is where you and your mate have a chance to keep that passion that you first started out with.

Your main goal should be to focus on your middle ground, a place where you both can dwell in synchronization.

It takes work and patience!

Now this is where the conflict enters. Because of the distractions you cause or the distractions that are already there, the energy becomes volatile. But if you give each other something that is constant; it makes relationships easier.

5 | Gay Pride

I guess back in the day, we treated homosexuality as something that happens in the neighbors family, or so and so's brother or sister.

In our time; undeniably it has even become a powerhouse in music, politics, and every facet of commerce in the world, and you cannot escape it. Trust me they will make you understand that they are here to stay.

What I have come to understand is that this ignorance of society's shift, is very detrimental to success. Because I work in downtown Atlanta. I have witnessed the gay pride parade, then the black gay pride parade.

Maybe a hundred thousand participants showed up. To tell the world that their life style is an expression of free speech.

You can't judge them out loud and you cannot change something that doesn't want to be changed. Almost three years ago Atlanta surpassed San Francisco as the gayest city in the US.

They will rebel, regroup, and keep coming back stronger. Yet they have something that I know is lacking in a lot of communities, organizations, and even the races.

Unity:

They look out for each other. They want to only marry their own. What the outside world don't get? This is like a global fraternity, which is unspoken. But very powerful, and the most important thing, is that they vote.

This shift is happening in nature, and nothing is as it was. They are changing the constitution of the United States. They are changing the doctrines of the church itself.

The world is revealing itself in a new light. The acceptance of things we don't understand; is becoming viable.

Like the acceptance that everything that is written in the bible is not gospel. It is merely the radical ideas of a population, of that particular time.

Something that really scares the elite. Is that knowledge and truth is becoming accessible to the average person, at an alarming rate.

The youth are learning more on their own, than what they are taught in school. They are learning things that was once forbidden to the average citizens.

Knowledge is power, and this generation and the generation before this one, are no longer accepting what was sold to them in the past.

This explosion of technology is happening too fast for the hierarchy too control. Is the time we're living in now, the secret that they have talked about in the bible? Or the prophecies of the age of human evolution?

That's why I'm so excited about our time, maybe we are the ones chosen to usher in the age of enlighgtment (Meaning information, internet, or the accessibility to the truth.)

6
The Hard Truth

This is the hard truth about some men: not all. But most about being unfaithful. The majority of the time when we as men are in a committed relationship, we truly know the female has not cheated yet. But the thought of us cheating has crossed our mind.

It is the atmosphere we can create, by having her think that we believe she is the one with those cheating thoughts. And that takes the pressure off of us.

It's psychological in its approach, and I will break it down so it can be understood. We as men are already suspect, due to our inherit nature of conquest, or being the man.

It's like a Mafia Don who seems to never get anything pinned on him. As time goes by. And there are too many wild fires. It becomes very hard to keep putting them out.

When all the accusations, the numbers on my phone, and the things the streets are telling her. Sink in her head, there's a problem.

I truly believe, we as men. When we commit, we really mean it at the time.

So in our defense: it's best to build a strategy in case there is a glitch. It's easier to level the playing field. This is really a defense strategy, on a mental street level.

So when the female does accuse you of something that you cannot give a believable explanation to.

And the old excuses aren't working, and don't sound credible anymore, it's time to reposition the players on the chess board.

7

What Women Never Understand

What women never understand is this. Men will never truly fess up to infidelity, unless the prosecutor has a rock solid case like DNA, videos, the TV show Cheaters, or her mother.

Before it ever gets that far, you throw salt in their game. You take the weight off of you. At least for a little while, so it can buy you some time.

You put the crime in her lap. Tell her you know she's cheating with whomever. And if you say it enough times even you will start to believe it.

Family members or best friends; make your accusation sound credible, because they spend time around each other.

So now you have taken your church going, good family, traditional girl, and made her into a manufactured whore.

That you married!

That's a good alibi for nonpayment of child support. The kid is not mine routine, or not being around, or why you cheated. Pretty much your overall emotional state. It's all so brilliant, and even the biggest players, criminals, and crack heads use it.

This is where it gets good! The woman spends so much time defending herself of not cheating.

Because she's trying to hold on to something that was a lie from the beginning, that she loses her grip on reality. Women let their emotions control their actions.

I probably should not be telling this; but fuck it, we live in a new age, and it's time to step up the game.

I make no apologies.

You have to understand this about men. It is not about the kids, or the friends, but mostly about the sex.

This is what really bothers men who are in a relationship. Is the thought of being with his wife or girlfriend, or significant other? Who does not want to have sex with him anymore, for whatever reason?

This will alter the status of your relationship...

I mean; for you to lay in bed, right next to him. And deny him of his God given right to fuck you senseless; and you still sleep better than you have in years. Is an abomination to a man's already frail ego?

The truth is this; just because we agree on something even if it is through marriage, boyfriend or girlfriend, an agreement is established.

Relationships take time, patience, and failure.

When you began missing what you have lost, and still feel that love. After all the slander, hurt words, revenge fuck, accusations, lies, and the kids have all moved on.

When the only thing that is left; is the ideal you first started out with. Then not only are you two together, you have forgiven the past.

When you understand you cannot change the past, but you can usher in a new future then something is renewed. With or without you!

That is an agreement of your common interest. A garden where something new can grow. You have to constantly be planting seeds.

That's the hard truth.

8

Trifling-Ass Women

This strategy cuts both ways, there are some very twisted women roaming this jungle we call earth. Women wonder why men go to the means they go through to separate themselves.

Women have a far better strategy in the justice system than men. Society automatically looks to the man for any delinquencies in the relationship until proven otherwise.

By law: women have to scientifically prove paternity, and legally ensure financial support. And in reality it has nothing to do with the female.

I call it post teen trauma. "He is supposed to take care of the kids, even if I'm not sure who the daddy is." When women become desperate they will chose the most available father. YOU!!

"Think about it?"

If you're in this predicament, and she has chosen you. There is no length she will not go, to make you look incompetent to your friends, family, kids, and the court of law. They will use that until it falls apart. Or until DNA proves that little nappy head kid isn't yours.

This is how fragile a man's vision is of his masculinity. I have known guys who have murder warrants out on them; but will call to ask me. "Have you seen who their ex is messing with"? Whether than worrying about the police that are looking for them.

It takes one women, or one bad relationship to leave a permanent tattoo on a man's brain.

Even if he is facing prison.

It takes one time of making a man believe that a child is his legacy. Or that he was part of the miracle of that one alcohol, drug, infested night with that women.

And then to deny him of his place in that child's life; is a devastating blow to any man's mental state.

To me this is felony abuse.

Then for the ill minded female, to contribute to the myth of a fair American trial in our justice system for that man is a travesty.

I mean for a female to assist in the court process, to ruin credibility, and degrade whatever manhood that he was trying to develop. You are basically helping with the genocide of men.

I realize some women do it without knowing what an important role they play. Then some know exactly what they're doing. Some of the men are straight takers in every way. Then through DNA; it is revealed the child wasn't his in the first place.

To me that is a massacre of a young man's chance to ever have a healthy or a meaningful place in every kid or relationship?

Every bond after this one, will be contaminated in his mind? If it doesn't break him.

9

Cherish

My personal story begins like this. One night while at work at the hospital, and making my rounds.

I was walking by a local night club in mid-town Atlanta. I was coming from the security post located on the corner of Peachtree St. and Linden Ave. Which is one block past Gladys's Knight Chicken and Waffle restaurant.

I was almost at the post of Peachtree and Pine Street. When I saw a young lady standing halfway on the sidewalk and halfway on the street. She said something to me that was completely out of the blue.

"Too bad you have to work tonight". She said with a sly smile.

I stopped for a moment, and focused my eyes on the voice, and what I saw was a moment frozen in time. A time when I was young and care free, and the world was mine.

I just stared at this petite brown skin lady that was wearing tight fitting jeans, and a brown shirt. She had a tattoo on her arm which read "Heaven Sent".

I was speechless, but I had to say something to redeem what I was feeling at that moment. So I deepened my voice and replied in my most distinguish voice.

"Yea, I'm trying to make this money; but I wish I could be doing what you're doing; enjoying life." She smiled and looked down at the concrete.

"You can if you really wanted to, but there is a sacrifice" She winked her eye. "The choice is always yours".

I put my head down and stared at the pavement, then I looked back up and said.

"You have a good night." I moved on to my next post and turned out the lights. I watched the cars and people bustle about Peachtree Street.

10

You Never Know What A Day Will Bring

The irony of life is this, after going almost a year, and not really being in a committed relationship. Mainly because of my work schedule and my recent past experience.

I met two women I really liked in the same day.

Later that same night I met a nurse at my job. She was in her early thirty's, divorced and sexy as hell. She had forgotten her ID badge and could not get into the parking deck.

I used my security badge to let her in. As I opened the door, her eyes met mine, and I guess it was one of those moments, that I call celestial timing.

Something clicked, I mean something, somewhere, agreed with this moment. I knew there was no turning back, and she also knew. She looked deeply into my eyes and held her stare, and before she shut her door she asked. "Are you new around here?'

"Yea... Sort of... I've been here, you just haven't been paying attention". I said.

"Well, I'm paying attention now", She looked at my name tag and repeated my name.

"Are you on Facebook?" She asked knowingly.

"I have an account, but I rarely use it".

"Check it later". She closed her door and drove off. I could hear some R Kelly music playing in her car. This lets me know, I'm not ready to settle down. When I got home, I checked my Facebook account.

Like I said when I first started this book. I had ideas and a direction. But as I go forward, I'm learning real life will write itself; and I'm just an interpreter.

The Conversation

Erin Garcia is a beautiful Hispanic female from Brooklyn New York. She recently lived in Texas. She relocated with her husband who she met in the military. His name is Jose and he works at Bank of America as a customer service representative.

Erin is a licensed pediatrician. She's a very ambitious young lady, with an attitude to match. She's always the best looking lady in the bunch, and she has the kind of cuteness that most men desire.

I mean she's 'homeboy' cool.

She would go to a place like Hooters or a strip club, and share a picture of beer with you. She would even offer to pay.

Cool!

I first met Erin one day when her husband had dropped her off at work. She had forgotten her security card. So she came to my post to ask if I would let her through the gate. On my way to open the gate she asked. "Are you the one who writes?"

I said "Yes".

"I heard you're really good, why do you still work here?'

"I'm too afraid to quit". I said.

"You will one day". We both smiled.

Erin is unique, and free spirited. And she's also my good friend. She is stuck in a marriage to an older man, who is still trying to run the streets.

I have met the guy briefly, but I could tell we had nothing in common.

I could tell by the way he drove up in his four door Saturn, with tinted windows, and blasting a song from Drake. It just didn't look right with the child seat sticking up from the back seat. I just laughed.

I knew Erin did not trust him. She knew he had other women, but she just could not prove it. She even called the TV show Cheaters, to get proof, but they never called her back.

She did the next best thing, she enlisted this older guy who was my supervisor name Benjamin Walters (Benny for short). Benny was a retired Atlanta Police Department Deputy, a divorcee, and he lived alone. He freelanced as a private detective.

He worked at the hospital as a security officer, because he said he was seeking a quieter life. She hired him to follow her husband, and to give her proof of his infidelity.

I knew nothing good was coming out of it.

Her best friend was a lady name Rachael who is married to my friend Romero. She is a white female who grew up in a predominately black neighborhood. She had two kids by two different black men.

Erin, Rachael and Benny schemed and plotted, on catching Erin's husband cheating. I just knew when it was all said and done, someone was going to get shot.

I explained to Erin and her white/black best friend Rachael about this book, and they agreed to give me a chapter. I never had an inclination of what was about to transpire, let's just say I couldn't make this stuff up. So I came up with a series of questions.

12 | Hooters

The reason I love Hooters is because it's close to my place, and my job. So I set up a date with Erin and Rachael. I brought my iPad as a recorder, and I let the ladies do what they do.

Talk without reservation.

All it took was a few shots of tequila, Buffalo wings, and a pitcher of beer. Reader: The only reason I included this particular segment in my book is because of the brutal honesty.

Maybe it was the tequila shots, the wings, or the atmosphere of the scadly dressed waitress, who paid our table a lot of attention.

Our waitress name was Vanessa. I guess she thought I was some interviewer for some magazine, or some author writing some relationship book, or a pimp. But for some reason it all worked out, and I got more than what I asked for.

13

"What Bugs You The Most About Men Today?"

"Where the fuck are they, and where is that man I thought that my father was? I take that back; because after getting to know how he really was. I see why my mother divorced him.

He couldn't keep a job, and he stayed behind on child support, but I love him, and I know at one time so did my mother". Erin set it off.

"Do you trust your man?" I added.

"No". They both replied.

"It's not that I don't trust him I don't trust this world" Erin finished up.

"If things don't work with you and your man, which more than likely will happen, and he finds someone else. Would you trust him to give you what you need for your kids?"

14 | The Rules of Engagement

"Hell Naw… You have to have a backup plan. My mother taught me the rules of engagement. It's like this; if he knocks me up then tries to leave, our relationship turns into a business." Erin said while pouring herself another glass of beer.

"What do you mean business?" I asked.

"Allow me to break this down for you, Mr. Author. My love, emotions, time, and my body cost. It's never free… nothing is free, freedom ain't even free… and this little get together ain't even free." They both laughed simultaneously again.

Our waitress Vanessa had brought a basket of Lemon Pepper and Buffalo chicken wings and placed them in the middle of the table. I said thank you, and she gave me a smile, and as soon as she walked away from the table.

Erin had a comment.

"That's the shit I'm talking about. Disrespect! I don't trust this world, that waitress is gaming on you. She sees one guy having wings and drinks with two fine ass females, and she figures there's money, or pimpin somewhere". Erin smiled and grabbed a lemon pepper wing.

"Now Erin; back to the business question?" I said trying to recapture her juvenile attention span.

"Oh my bag… let me finish. Just because they won't put your marriage on paper, ya know marriage license. There are other papers he can be put on. Like child support, alimony, or hush money, or the just because he feels like he owes you something money."

"Hush money, or he owes you something?" Please explain I semi pleaded.

"Gladly... You see hush money are those little secrets he doesn't want the world to know. I believe all men do things they not supposed to, and they will keep doing it until they get caught".

"Things like what?"

"Things... like, they can't fuck... little dick... fakin ballin... undercover gay, or married. You know they aren't the big man their home boys think they are, or they ain't the man they thought they were." She said with a sneer.

"How do you know their frontin a lifestyle or image?" I asked.

"Oh... we know from the jump, or we have an idea. You see the way he invest in me, I invest in him. I do my research. My body, my time, my kid, and me putting aside my dreams. It's not cool when it's not real.

Hell yea! We are peepin game from the jump. Well at least some of us are." "(Cough)." She looked at Rachael.

I was starting to really feel good about this book, but you would be surprised how much a person changes after a few shots and some wings. I let Erin talk, besides I couldn't shut her up.

"You see Mr. Writer; this day and age is twisted. 'Back in the day' all you had to worry about was your home girl, the slut up the street, or him spending money at the strip clubs."

"Yea, what changed?" I asked.

"What changed? Now a days we have to worry about him liking my little brother, or one of his so called home boys, or he is seriously on the down low." Erin said becoming very angry.

The waitress walked by the table just checking on us, and Erin gave her a mean look. I moved my I- pad closer so I would not miss anything. I knew Erin was upset.

"Remember those days when a guy says "Oh I was just out with the boys kickin it". Now a days every female is thinking twice about that statement.

A real woman knows when something ain't right. But it's up to her if she chooses to ignore the signs, which eventually, will blow up in her face.

She will be left alone, broke, and with a kid that looks just like his trifling ass. That reminds her of a love that was never hers in the first place.

That's why you have to have street collateral".

15 | Street Collateral

"Street Collateral?" I asked.

"You damm right! You put it on paper. Take it to the feds, child support, and hush money, whatever. I'll be nice and a lady, but I make sure it's all documented in the courts.

So when he acts up, I'll act up! I'll wait, fuck him, and praise him, but when that times comes around. I will be ready." Erin finished the last of the pitcher of beer. Now she's looking for that same waitress she doesn't like.

"I feel sorry for your man." I said trying to add fuel to her rant.

"So do I". Erin barked back from across the table.

16 | Why Black Men End Up With White Women

I realized Rachael was suspiciously silent. I had ordered her an Apple Martini, and she was sipping on her drink. She was silently taking in the whole conversation. So I turned my attention towards her.

"Rachael; what bothers you the most about men?' I asked.

Rachael looked up at me from across the table and very calmly said.

"I love black men. I like them short, light, dark, or broke. I just do. I just like the feeling of having the black struggle. I want my kids to be black.

I have been culturally abandoned by my own race, family, and friends. White people don't like me, and black girls don't like me because I have a nice ass." She grinned and took a sip.

That's why you choose black men". I asked.

"No, they choose me, they speak first, and they feel comfortable around me, I make them feel like a man."

"Your saying some black women, don't make a man feel like a man". I asked.

"Not all but some, but only when it's convenient for them." She said without looking up.

"Ok… What if your black man cheats on you?" I asked.

"I really don't care, if my man leaves me, cheats on me, or runs off with another women or man. I have my kids, and I have my own money." She blushed.

"You mean, if your man starts to act crazy, you wouldn't do what Erin calls the "Rules of Engagement." I asked.

"I don't know… The way I see it, with my husband I have now. When we first hooked up he was sleeping with my home girl, and they broke up." She took a deep breath.

"So I got him in a foul way from the beginning. I knew he wasn't about shit then, and I know he ain't about shit now. You reap what you sow." She said and continued sipping on her drink.

"Fuck that!". Erin yelled. I know a lawyer who will file your papers for a piece of ass, and you can throw in some domestic battery, or emotional trauma, put it on paper. If he drinks or smokes weed, or he's on probation or pending, hit him up."

"Like I said Erin I feel sorry for your man". I stated.

She laughed and said. "I'm getting fucked up" She waved down our waitress who she doesn't like, and we ordered another round of shots and another pitcher of beer.

17 | Obama and Relationships

"This administration is ruining our men. If a man has an Obama phone, (Free phone for the needy). Then that means he gets food stamps, which pretty much means he ain't workin". Erin said with that same sneer,

"Well maybe he has had a run of bad luck" I said trying to appease the hostility I saw brewing in her pretty eyes.

"I don't care; we can have sex; but that's it". She said then glancing over at Rachael who was sipping on her drink, and looking down her cell phone.

"Look I have to support the men who are trying to make a come-up. The way I see it, we're all in this together, love it or hate it. This is our world, our time, and our mess.

Everyone deserves the opportunity to make a comeback. Our house may be dysfunctional but it is our duty to keep the lights on, and to make sure that our family is safe." I said my peace, and for once the table was quiet.

I was really interested in Rachael's mind set. Her attitude towards life was new to me. She was a very attractive white girl, with a black girl's body.

There was something about the way she put everything in perspective that appealed to me. I knew this was good for the book. I will pursue this in a later chapter, or Everything Volume 2.

18 | Sugar daddies

Benny

"HAVE YOU EVER SAT BACK AND WATCHED PEOPLE?" I mean watch them without their knowledge, and no I'm not talking about a 'peeping tom'. But just observing people in their natural habitat.

Them being themselves:

People are very interesting; they are stories within themselves. They are thrillers writing their own novels. One particular Friday, I was maintaining my post that is located on the corner of Peachtree Street and Linden Street.

I happen to catch a glimpse of Lieutenant Benny. He was walking one of the nurses to her car. At my angle I could see them but they couldn't see me, and I decided to write down exactly what I saw.

From my perception. I could tell, she was thanking him for taking time out of his busy schedule to escort her to her car.

Then I could tell by his gestures, he was telling her how much he doesn't mind, and him replying "This is just who he is, and what he does, he serves others."

I can read this like a book.

There was something predatory about the way he would look at her through his dark sunglasses. I mean he was really eyeing her from head to toe. It's the way a criminal cases a bank. He was scheming on her.

I know.

He would then adjust his belt as if he was getting ready for something very important. Then adjust his radio signal button as if he just received some urgent transmission. He would look around as if he was protecting her from any eminent danger.

I knew better cause I'm on the same frequency and there's nothing happening.

A strange feeling came over me, that he wasn't being the Good-Samaritan he portrayed. But this man was casing her. I could only imagine the subtle conversation he engages with her. He was looking for a way in.

"A Sugar Daddy way in."

From the corner of his eye I could see him looking at her car tires, and the inside of her car.

See you can tell a lot about a person by just observing the obvious. I mean by the way the inside of her car looks. Are there any children toys, gym bag, books?

You look for any immature men stuff like speakers in the back, tinted windows, or those get rich quick books on the floor of the backseat. But Benny had already saw his angle.

I could decipher that he was asking her about her tires.

"Have you checked the pressure on your tires lately, because this one in the back looks low"? Then of course she will look at the tire, and have no clue of what he's talking about, and say. "No"

"Does your man… husband, does he know about cars?"

"No, we are separated". She replies, embarrassed that she didn't noticed the tire.

That's it he's in, and if she doesn't catch on, he's got her. This is how **Sugar Daddies** operate. Then he'll say. "I'll check them for you, maybe tomorrow, the last thing you need is to be on Interstate 285, and have a flat". He just established a father figure, and trust relationship.

Believe it or not; women, especially single women, or women with problem baby daddies go for that. Because right now that's what their looking for in a man. One that isn't absent.

For Benny and at his age of fifty-five, it was brilliant, because even though he was a creep, and goofy. He was financially stable, and to many women that is an aphrodisiac.

After waiting and watching the nurse drive off, with her 'too low' tire permeating her brain. Benny coolly walked by my Security booth. Once again he had that grin, and with that one gold tooth gleaming in the sun.

That said. "I'm the man, yea I still got it". He stopped right in front of the security booth, and he peered in the window. He was eyeing me through his Ray Bans sunglasses.

"Have you seen Erin"?

"Naw I haven't been looking for her". I replied.

"Well make sure you're watching your post, and make sure your walkie isn't dead.

(The battery on my walkie talkie).

Then he just smiled and walk towards the entrance of the hospital.

First why would he ask me about Erin? Was he trying to prove something, or give me some kind of old school hint? Since he was my superior I focused on other things, but I knew there was more to this story.

19

The Round Table

A month has passed, and like we promised we met up at Hooters again. Erin Rachael, and I. I used my phone as a voice recorder. This time I ordered a round of frozen margaritas, with a side of Patron tequila shots.

We took the shots together, then I pressed record.

First question: "Ladies what has changed since our last session?" Of course Erin spoke first.

"That motherfucker has a bitch, and I'm all fucked up". She said slightly raising her voice.

"Who, your husband?" I asked, and she nodded.

"You got all this from Benny?" She nodded again.

"Yes he's better than those Cheater's detectives, and he even has pictures, and video". She said while grabbing a chicken wing, and licking her fingers.

"How does that make you feel?" I asked.

"Revenge", she mumbled, and her eyes glared at me like I was the one she was after.

I noticed the whole time we were talking, Rachael stared at every word that came from Erin's mouth. I didn't want to leave Rachael out before Erin hogged the whole session.

I was curious why she was so absorbed with what Erin was saying. So I asked her the same question. This time they both looked at each other, then they both looked at me.

"So what's new?" I asked again.

"Tell him… Tell him that your man ain't shit either, tell him about us". Erin blurted out.

"What about ya'll?" I waited and that's when Erin's phone went off. She checked it immediately, and excused herself from the table. Which left me and Rachael alone, with record still on.

Why A White Girl Could Get Any Black Man

I guess the secret is not having Erin around, to get Rachael to talk. And did she talk. This is blunt and it might hurt some feelings but, this is our time.

"Rachael Raw. R&R"

"Most black girls hate me, and I personally don't have a shortage of men".

"Black men". I interrupted.

"Yes, you have no idea the men who try to fuck me on the sly, or the women who try the same. I'm not a whore, but things just happen"

"What happens, you just always end up on your back?" I chimed in.

"No." She giggled.

"I might be white on the outside, but on the inside I'm black, and probably gay, and a racist against both races.

I have a kids that will be categorized as being black by a society that has never grown up. This is my life and I'm cool with it."

"How do you feel about the white lady from the NAACP posing as a black woman all these years?" I asked.

"What's the big deal; if she's doing what makes her happy, and her job, who gives a fuck? She shouldn't care; because when all the smoke clears all she will be left with is herself to deal with. And that is the person she should be making happy".

"Nice answer. Do you believe there is a shortage of good men?" I asked.

"No… you have to get one and work with him, try and mold them. Understand that the majority of them were raised by single women. When there is no father around they miss out on the being a man experience.

Expect them to cheat, and hurt you, that way you won't be so surprised when it happens," She replied while taking sips on her drink.

"Which means you never ever truly trust, and doesn't that lower your standards?" I asked.

"I guess not, and when it comes to my kids, everything else falls second; even my hurt over some man." She said.

"I know some black women who have done the impossible, they have survived, and raised their kids, with minimal help from their families or the baby fathers."

"What advice would you give your sisters out there?" I asked.

"OK… Those women are my heroes. But If you're always chasing money, it will forever be running from you. Black women want men to take care of their every need, but the truth is, those days are gone; if they ever really existed. It's like the female's mentality has evolved sideways."

"Please explain?'

"I feel men want you to work just as hard as they do, maybe harder, and I think I'm right". She gave a confident grin.

"My grandma once told me, when I was younger. In this world in order for a black man to feel secure in a relationship.

"The woman will have to love you more." The pressure from this society, and our world dictates it. The playing field is not level. Does that make sense to you?" I asked.

"Yea, but it's not just black men these days, all men are struggling. Nobody is safe, not the rich, rappers, millionaires, no one is immune to getting their heart crushed. It's all fixed." Rachael blushed again.

"So that's why you're more patient, towards your man?" I added.

"Yes, the way I see it; we have a kid together, and if he fails we fail. I guess that is my sacrifice in the game, and for my son. I don't want him to grow up without a father. So yes! I put up with more, and I work harder."

"Now, not to back track, why do you feel you might be gay".

"The affection I don't get at home, I still crave even more these days, because I have more on my plate. I'm human and I want to be loved. Lately I've been getting that attention from what and who I've been around, like my friends."

"Maybe Erin". She didn't answer the question.

Even though I found myself attracted to both Erin and Rachael. This situation was bigger than me, and besides, I needed to stay focused on this book.

Erin came back to the table just to tell us she had something very important to take care of, and she left. I finished up with Rachael, and she left.

I was left alone at the table with a half pitcher of beer, a basket of wings and the check. I called my editor Kayla before I went home. I got her answering service, but I didn't leave a message. I knew she would call back when she had time.

21

Charleston Massacre

Thursday-6-2015

The way I'm writing this book is unorthodox, but I insist on staying current with events. Two things occupied my thoughts.

In Charleston South Carolina at the Emmanuel African Methodist Episcopal Church, some members were gathered for a bible study. A young white man name Dylan Roof opened fire and killed nine members even the pastor, who were religious people, who all welcomed him with open arms.

I must speak on this.

This confirms my theory about everything. No one is safe, nothing is sacred anymore, not even church.

Live your life, follow your dreams, and don't let your regrets have more space in your life than your success.

Take a chance, say what's on your mind, and free yourself. Let go of the things, which have been keeping you from discovering the person you can and will become.

The world is yours. Every day is another chance to fix what you can. Burn as less bridges in life that you can help. Some of them you can't help, but you try and keep, and build the roads that matter. Because you never know when you might have to cross them again.

So I tell you to hold on, life is so precious, and it can be taken at any moment.

My prayers goes out to the friends and families of those who have lost loved ones, and my heart goes out to those who have the strength to move on. Please stay strong your day will come.

22

My Analogy

Rachael's mentality is subtle, but dangerous. Let me tell you why. All the bad things that have happened to her, she has absorbed like a sponge.

She has taken in more and more bullshit until her burdens become so heavy, and nothing can fill that place. Until someone or something comes along and squeezes the sponge and the rain comes, and she can't control the water, and everything gets wet.

I hate to admit it: but I understand this way of thinking. It is a time bomb for suicide. It's like a boxing match where a fighter takes a beating without even trying to win.

Somewhere deep down inside they feel they deserve the pain. Instead of deserving to be happy. So they build up a shield, "No matter what you throw at me, you cannot hurt me, this is no worse than the things that have already been done to me."

Even though I know this analogy is self-destructive. I have done it too. And I will probably do it again in the future.

23 | The Unspoken

I called Erin the next day and set up a new date. I wanted to tackle a subject that is so prevalent in our society. So we met up again for dinner. This subject happens so much in our life time that many times it goes unchecked, but I said this book was going to be brutal. I knew Erin wouldn't hesitate to speak her mind.

"Has anyone ever taken your body without your permission?" I asked.

"What... rape, assault," Erin chimed in first like I knew she would.

"Yea... believe it or not it affects every relationship you will ever have. From lovers, or friends, and you will have major trust issues especially, if it was a family member or someone you trusted." I asked making this meeting more personal.

"I thought we were talking about relationships and life in this day and age, these are things that happen a long time ago?" Erin asked. They both shook their heads.

"Yea... but I bet you remember it like it was yesterday, and that person and that moment has left a tattoo on your brain, and it affects every relationship you will ever have." I said.

Everyone was silent.

I wanted this project to be fun, but I wanted it to be brutally blunt. Yet I didn't want to lose the trust I had with them before I finished this book. So I did the next best thing, I ordered another round of shots.

I waited until the subject was brought up again. I waited for someone, to speak first and I knew it would be Erin, but it wasn't; it was Racheal.

"I was raped by my uncle when I was twelve. The first time I really didn't know what to do. My father wasn't around and he was helping my mother with my brother and me".

"You never told anyone?" I asked.

"He was my father's brother, and my mom let him live with us. And she adored him because he was doing what my father wasn't for us". Rachael said.

"Did you tell your mom?" I asked.

"I didn't know how to, it happened one more time, and I let him. My uncle said I was helping him. We didn't have a car, and my mom needed a ride to her job, and he had the only car.

She was a single mother and we lived in a gang and drug infested neighborhood." She said as her eyes were becoming watery.

I really didn't want to pursue this, but I recognized a pattern, even at her young age, she allowed herself to be hurt. I could tell by the drop in her tone, and her not looking me in my eyes; that I struck something deep. I didn't want to ask this next question but she answered it for me.

"I guess you want to know how my situation: ended for your book?" I didn't respond I just looked at her.

"When I was 14 my mother had him arrested for raping her. He did 4 years in prison. I never said a word until now. My father; to this day blames my mother for letting my uncle live with us in the first place." Rachael said.

She was looking down at the table, but I had one more question to ask for closure.

"Does it bother you to this day?"

"Yes... I'm afraid to be alone, and I'm afraid for my kids, I 'm very protective."

Erin grabbed her hand, then she grabbed her shot glass, and pushed Rachael's in her hand and they both took a shot. Erin then wiped her mouth and looked at me and said".

"I'm raped every time my lame ass husband tries to fuck me, it stop being consensual a while ago." I turned off the recorder and I took a shot, and poured myself a glass of beer.

24

Cherish 7

I have an off-and-on relationship, with a lady name Bethany and everything is gravy, (I mean no problems.) We haven't had one argument, and I'm worried. Our schedules are almost identical, so our time is shared. She respects the time I need to reflect and write, and it's what really makes me happy.

Lately she has been hinting at us getting a place together. You know, to save money since we already spend so much time together. I can tell she's getting serious. And I thought I was too until one Monday while making my rounds at work.

I was walking through the lobby of Admissions that's on Linden Street. When I heard a familiar voice. I looked over from the information desk, and there was Sarah the day receptionist busy on the phone, but I knew I had heard Cherishes voice.

I looked to my left and sitting in the front row was Cherish, sitting with an elderly lady with an IV connected to her arm.

Cherish was wearing black jeans with a light silver Belk and a gray tank top. I could clearly see her tattoo which said 'Heaven sent' on her arm.

"Hello stranger". She said while gazing up at me.

"Hi… Where have you been?" I said, clearly surprised to see her.

"I've always been, where I've always been". She smiled.

"And who is this?" I asked about the elderly lady sitting and holding her hand.

"This is my grandma Nettie Mae, and she's an outpatient here at your hospital.

I knew right then and there I should have said hello; and do the formal introductions. "(You know I hope everything's fine, good seein you again.)" And I should have walked away, but I didn't. I invited them to the cafeteria for some coffee.

I tried to convince myself that this was an innocent gesture, and there nothing to this; I'm just being cool. Yea I'm cool and Cherish is fine.

And she knew it.

I know this will sound funny but, here it goes. It wasn't Cherish and her good looks, or her quick wit that won me over. It was her grandma Nettie Mae. We talked my whole break and Cherish sat there and listened.

I love wisdom, and I try to capture it.

This lady was filled with a spirit that moved me. She had to be one of the sweetest ladies I have ever met, and her granddaughter just sweetened the package.

I began feeling guilty, and I don't know why, I haven't cheated physically, but my mind was all in. So for the next week I met them in the cafeteria for my breaks. I soon realized I was looking forward to meeting with them more than I was with Bethany.

The last day of her therapy, we were having coffee at our table by the window.

When I heard a chair scrape the floor, and I heard a thud. Erin had pulled a chair, and sat down at the table with us and introduced herself. I just stared at her from across the table.

"Hi, I'm Erin". She said as she reached across the table to shake everyone's hands.

"I'm a good friend of Bobby's". (That's my nick name in Atlanta). She said as she got comfortable in her seat.

We all sat silent for one uncomfortable minute, and I broke the silence. "Sorry but we were on our way out." So I excused all of us and left Erin sitting by herself.

25

Demented

This chapter really bothered me, but I knew it needed to be written. I knew something was wrong in Erin's life. So I'll start where I first discerned it.

This is a new age predator. This one is different, a true chameleon in sorts because he hides behind, what I would call uniforms of prestige and trust.

He is usually a person with a badge or a title, or someone who is elevated in society for whatever reason.

Some of the memories I have are disturbing, but when it was going on I really thought all this was normal. Now when I look back I realize it was criminal. Some of these men I know are married, with careers, and children.

I guess too much time has gone by, or people have forgotten, and some of these women are still with the ones who had victimized them. But in all fairness some women knew they were being preyed upon.

In reality these same men should have been locked up, and prosecuted and been a member of the sexual predator's club.

Maybe it's just my conscience, and it's too late. But every time, and throughout my life, when I encounter this type of personality, I cringe.

I can never escape the way I feel today. That's why I took extra care on this chapter, and I hope it helps someone.

In our time we live in a parallel dimension of the way things used to be. I mean the attitude, money, music, the game, even the players have changed. Even drugs have evolved, only the drama and the faces remain the same.

Young ladies growing up in this era, should be very afraid, and so should the parents. Which I hope, some will read this book. After all these years the courts are just now starting to understand the different levels rape can occur?

I am here to tell you there are a lot of these young girls out here who have multiple babies at a young age. You know so- and- so's child, the honor student, the preacher's daughter, or Miss Avery's granddaughter.

Some of these kids are what I term, "I want to be down girls". None of these girls intended to have two to three kids before they turned twenty-one.

Allow me to elaborate, a good female friend of mine, once told me about her baby daddies and her two kids. We were talking one night over drinks.

"Ya know I love my kids". She blurted out of the blue.

"OK" I replied. Something told me to turn on the recorder on my phone. I told her I was recording and she said. "Fuck it! Let's do it".

"Do you even remember the night you first got pregnant?" I asked.

"No, honestly; I was with my good friend Tameka, and we decided to hang out with this guy she knew. We went over his house to smoke weed and that was supposed to be it.

I met this guy who convinced me to take this drink he prepared for me, and smoke this 'dope- ass weed'. After that I don't remember what happened." She replied.

"Do you remember where you were, and can you remember taking off your clothes?' I asked.

"Sort of". She really had a confused look on her face.

"So what happened?" I asked.

"Basically I was raped?" A tear formed in her eye.

"I was eighteen, and that year instead of going to college I had my first kid. I was embarrassed, and my mom felt I was being promiscuous".

"What about the guy?" I then asked.

"After that I couldn't get rid of him. I didn't believe in an abortion, and I would not have never gotten with a guy like that. I would have gone to college." She replied.

"So where is the guy at now?" I asked.

"He's my husband". She stated.

I ended this session because I knew her man.

26 | Red Flags

These are those things, or moments that we choose to ignore, even though we know what's best for us. It's the things that are not so blatant in the beginning, but has always been present, dwelling just beneath the surface.

"God gives us the wisdom" and he does all the time. We just choose not to listen, we choose what's convenient for our emotions at the time. Not really concerned about the future that lies just over the horizon.

That's why it's so easy to pick that good looking person with that nice job, nice car, and big house. It's easy to choose things someone already worked for and earned. The hard way is to invest and build with someone, where we both have a stake in our future. So when we fall, we look for the easy road, and then try to hitch a ride on one of those fast moving cars.

Time wears down even the hardest hearts, and desperation leads us to necessity but it's always better to go in with aces in your deck too.

I don't care how much money you make this fact is a life lesson. If you don't understand money you will never have or keep money, and that is one of the biggest red flags.

Word to the wise, don't make plans that you cannot afford, and don't make plans for other people's money. Nothing is free not even freedom. In one way or the other we will pay for the things we want, and that goes both ways for men and women.

27

Romero

(Rachael's Husband)

My friend Romero is Rachael's husband, and works for Atlanta Police Department, and he has worked for the city for more than six years, and he is of Indian descent, but he looks and acts black. He only dates white women or real light skin females.

He's a good looking guy and he frequents all the online dating sites, like Facebook, twitter, etc. You probably have seen his type.

He grew up in Decatur, Georgia, and he went to Redan High School, but his family is from Dubai. He has served in our military, and he is a top notch officer. I have witnessed certain things about him, which have begun to be unsettling.

My analogy doesn't count for much, but the older I'm getting, I can nail things with an uncanny precision.

My wisdom is becoming more aware that things on the surface are not what they seem. I think my talent is making the complicated simple, or should I say understandable for the average person.

Romero enjoys power that's why he chooses certain professions. He's only comfortable in any relationship when he has the upper hand, or authority.

I have been around him, and his wife and kids. I personally know that he cheats every chance he gets. What really attracts him, is seeing a female in a disadvantage state. I mean he thrives on that.

This is the medium that he exist in, he likes women drunk, dependent, or who has a substance abuse problem. These type of men prey on single women. Especially ones who have kids with no man present, who are lonely, or just stupid.

And I really mean the last one.

In my time I have dated, or been friends with some of the most intellectually educated high paid females in the work force. But the majority of these women lacked a very essential element.

"(Common Sense)."

Their lives on the outside is flawless, but the inside is a wreck.

Back in the day Romero was that kid that always had weed, and a car, and a place to crash. His motivation for having those things were not honorable. Especially towards women.

He had a two parent household, and lived in a nice neighborhood, but he choose to hang out with us. I mean us single parent welfare savvy generation kids.

Even when we were younger. I never noticed it until a lady friend explained to me what he does, and why he does.

Growing up; Romero loved to get everyone high, or drunk, or both. But what he really liked was seeing women in a compromising situation, I mean he got off on it.

She explained to me that in order for him to feel comfortable. He has to be in control, or has to be needed, or it doesn't work. This is how he would make them feel obligated to have sex.

"WOW" I use to think he was helping these women out, until I heard him speaking on this subject one day. I witnessed the way he would treat the ones around him who needed him.

Then it began to sink in, that's why he treated his wife like shit. It's probably an insecurity that began as a child, and it manifested as he grew.

That's why this Bill Cosby situation sounds so familiar. I can't count how many parties, dates, or times when we were just hanging out with females.

Afterwards I would hear the same jargon from these women, and why they would stop messing with him. I never truly understood until now, and after talking to Rachael. It's just sad it took all this time, and kids for her to become awake.

I remember if a female played hard to get, he was patient, and he would be there for her as if he was her man. He would be that friend, a shoulder to cry on; until he could get her dependency.

Then he could be himself. He would began to resent the lady, and everything she represented. I can only write this because I have witnessed it happen time and time again.

Let's get to the here and now. The things he has done in his past is slowly creeping up on him. His game isn't so easy, or women are wiser in this day and age.

But he still has not learned. I guess that's why his wife is divorcing him, and taking the kids. She has taken her collateral. He was a young Benny.

28

The Man Code

I couldn't decide if I was beginning to get serious about Bethany. I did not want things to move too fast. This book was starting to take precedent because I was beginning to love writing it.

Someone once told me, that there is no such thing as luck. Life is about patience, timing, and preparation, and I'm beginning to believe that. I recognize the things that are happening to me.

God is always part of my life, even though I slip and fall, I never stray too far, and I mean my faith is always dominate.

Work tonight is quiet. The usuals are out and about, and my mind is easy like the city, and I'm praying for morning.

I have developed a new found respect for the ones who work in Health Care, Public Service, or anything serving others, the task is a humility job. I guess the rewards are true to their nature.

It's six am, and the first wave of nurses who work third shift are leaving. No one is smiling from the ER. They have that look that soldiers have, who have just come from a gruesome battle and they are thinking in their mind.

"What the fuck have I gotten myself into, or did I really just witness what happened last night? Will I ever be the same? Should I consider another profession?"

I empathize with them. Even I don't think I could take seeing all that blood.

I look over at the gate on G lot, and I see Erin and Benny walking towards my post. I knew what they were talking about, and I could tell Erin was very upset.

Even when she's angry she still looks cute. Benny walks her to her car, and she drives off. He then walks up to my post looking like a guilty plumber. First he didn't say a word. He just stood there with his hands in his pocket. So I broke the silence.

"So what's up lieutenant?"

"Oh… nothing just handling my business". He smirked.

He began rubbing the palm of his hands together, and we both stood silent on the sidewalk. As we both watched Erin drive by. I asked something that I probably shouldn't of, but I did.

"So, how's the P.I. business going?'

"It has its fringe benefits". He did that grin again, and rubbed his hands. "Her husband is cheating on her in the worst way." Benny said with that same grin.

"You know this is a very dangerous situation, and you gave her proof." I said.

"Yea." He smirked again.

"This is where you let it go". I replied.

"When I get the rest of my payment". He said confidently.I

"How do you plan on that?' I asked.

"I've got my ways".

Reader, I started this book with good intentions, it was supposed to be about our time, here and now, but things never happen the way you want, especially when writing a book as things happen.

29 | The Last of The Mohicans

It's been three months since we had our last session. It took some time to get Erin and Rachael together again. We met at The Georgia Juke Joint, which is located down town on Peachtree Street.

I ordered some drinks, and appetizers, and I set my iPad to record. Like I already knew, Erin's plan to set up her husband backfired. Her husband found out about her, under cover moves, and he decided to move out and file for a divorce.

I waited for the food and drinks before I asked my first question.

AFTER MATH

"What are you going to do now"? I asked, directing the question to Erin.

'My husband is leaving me because he thinks I'm sleeping with Benny." She said solemnly.

"Well are you sleeping with him"? I asked.

"He was helping me". She never answered the question.

"I knew nothing good was going to come out of this, you can't be playing with people's lives" I said.

"I know… I know…" She mumbled.

Rachael sat across the table and was suspiciously quiet. She was sippin on her drink, and picking at her food.

"So did you sleep with Benny"? I asked again

"Not quite but I am sleeping with her". She said while looking at Rachael.

Rachael continued to look down at the table.

"Is this true Rachael?" I asked, and she nodded her head.

"Men are dogs, and we're tired of the bullshit, at least Erin and I have something in common." She replied angrily. Then they kissed passionately.

I was taken back, I realized my other questions are now irrelevant, but I thought about something I had said. "You have be very careful when it comes to dealing with other people's lives. I knew it was my turn to be honest with Bethany."

30

My Positivity Outweighs My Negativity

I find happiness in the least likely places. I search for that peace that was promised to me. Maybe that peace is heaven, or a state of existence. A place where the troubles of this world don't worry you or hold you down. A place where fear and doubt has no refuge.

In my peace, I am anything and everything, yet nothing compared to the whole scheme of things. I have the knowledge of knowing I can and have made a difference to someone, somewhere.

Maybe that's where immortality lies. That piece of you that remains, with each and every person you encounter. Something about you lingering in time and space, so that others can absorb the energy you held, for your time on this earth.

This fuels the energy so that your light grows stronger, and brighter. It manifest itself in the very cells, nucleus, and even the basic building blocks of matter itself. You become one with the universe, and its energy attracts others like you. How powerful you truly are.

Make your life count!

This journey is a way of realizing our freedom. With our mind and imagination, we are bound to no one, or nothing. If you think it, you can become your purpose on this earth.

Which means my spirit is free, but my flesh can be hurt, and my soul lies somewhere in between, in an uncertain limbo. "Could that limbo be earth?"

One other thing that is constant is pain, and it comes on all levels. Some people suffer from the pain of just living. Others have handicaps that are not physical, but many are mental, which is a lot of times worse.

INTERVENTION

Yesterday they finally buried Bobbi Christina Brown. I feel the whole situation is so sad. People say she didn't have a chance and neither did her mom Whitney Houston.

The way I see it we all have choices, and after a certain age we are responsible for our own upbringing. I know everyone who was in their circle are wondering what role they played, and if maybe they could of saved both the lives.

31

Going Steady

Bethany's mother has been calling me on a regular basis, like were such good friends. It seems like she wants to ask me something, but doesn't know how to approach me.

The closer Bethany tries to get to me I find myself pulling away. I believe it has something to do with my childhood.

I never realized it until I would get into a committed relationship, and things are going well.

This is not a race thing, but a cultural thing and this is how a person's upbringing effects a young male's psychological state of mind.

A child who is growing up with no consistent male figure, or losing the ones who did matter in their life. They are denied a love that a women cannot give. That's why a male should be present in the growth of a child.

This manifest a defense mechanism within that child that triggers an emotion, of not allowing someone in your life. It hurts worse as a kid. And it's called survival even at that young tender age.

No one wants their heart broken.

If this happens enough times in someone's life, then you can't exist in a healthy relationship when you never knew how one is supposed to be.

Some men act the way they do out of pride. Some do it without even thinking. The only relationship they know is what they see on TV, music videos, or the sorry ass men their mothers chose. Some think that is normal, or some men just don't give a fuck, and they are just grimy.

They see the way men treated their mother when they were kids. They would listen to the conversations the women would have with each other.

Children absorb everything like a sponge, and basically most of the cheating, and abuse, is started by society's interference. Things like social media, music, and someone feeling like they are being 'disrespected.'

What a good word to summarize the initial reason why so many men are locked up today.

"Disrespecting"

32

"You Disrespecting Me!"

This is the Downfall of Generations

Men are so obsessed with someone disrespecting them. They feel it makes them look weak or gay, and this where the insecurity lies. Now tie that in with a whole lot of drugs, welfare, and firearms and you can see how bad this could get.

People have committed murder because they felt they were being disrespected. These are the egos that a lot of women choose to define their man, and their kids.

Do you know how hard it is to keep making a person feel like they are the most respected man on the block, when as days goes by your losing respect for him, and he knows it.

Try not returning his phone calls, not fucking him, understand this is the mentality you chose, because you might personally be going through your own thing. And by you not giving him his props twenty four seven, is disrespectful. It's very hard having to always make someone feel secure about themselves.

Insecurity gets old quick.

33 | Economics

The powers that be, suggest that this economy is just going through a phase, an adolescence in nation years. They say that eventually things will be the way it was. Like some political party is going to be the genius cell, to somehow put a magical jump to a nation that's on life support.

This is what they are not telling you. And I will make it simple so all can understand. This is what the elite, government, and known economists have known for years. The end of the middle class is here and now. Period!

Small businesses are almost obsolete. The fast jobs of the past are that the past, and they're not coming back. The needed services can be completed without all that human baggage that comes along with it.

Things like medical insurance, overtime. Sick leave, pensions. A computer doesn't tell your boss, no or you're an ass.

The jobs as we knew are fairy tales, of a day and age, when a household could support a family without government assistant. When hard work and sweat was your testimony. The topic of conversation at family barbecues, weddings, and knowing you own your house, and you can pass it on to your kids.

Jobs like those are as rare as Aids and Ebola is these days. We are living in a transitional turning. The target has a certain demographic, black males.

I believe this is by design.

They are systematically creating a society where there are two classes. The rest are caught in limbo, and governments around the world don't know what to do with this population.

Poverty is witnessing a new face, with other motives. Trust me, there are people out there who knew this was going to happen, and they know things are going to get worse. In order to keep their prestige the politicians have kept selling the American dream, all the while knowing it has turned into a night mare.

The way I see it; we were too busy with the culture explosion of the gangsta era, that we never saw it coming. Now you're too old to be a thug, or have too many felonies to get a decent job. Even the drug game is pretty much obsolete.

This is the hard truth, too many young men are not making it, and some are born lost, but there's hope, you can be found again.

34 | The Break up

I've been dating Bethany off and on for a year, and I know what she's thinking. Today I ended our relationship. My mind is on other things. For no particular reason I started thinking about the things that she does that bothers me.

When we're out together, she is more concerned with, who I'm looking at. When I'm not on the phone with her. She wants to know where I'm located, or who I'm with. She wants to know why I don't call her back in ample time.

These things are subtle, and cute in the beginning. You have to understand this. As minute as they are now, these are the warning signs.

These are signs of trust issues, and it will escalate, and this goes for both men and women.

Whenever she acts like this, I find myself slipping away or I find myself thinking of Cherish. Maybe she would act the same, these things permeate my thoughts.

How can a relationship be exclusive when my mind is somewhere else? Even if I haven't cheated physically, I'm cheating in my subconscious. Even though I really care for Beth.

I knew she had a career, some money, and a house. What scared me the most is that she made herself into a female that thinks she never needs a man.

How can you have a mindset of having a family, when every move you make is a plan B, for life? Preparing to be without a man, or you growing old alone?

This is the deliberate massacre of the structured family that was here at one time.

Society's pressure, media, and welfare, has systematically destroyed the family unit. We have females who really think they can be the father and the mother, and look what that has produced.

I wanted to feel like my beginnings, my family, and me being something important, was the only way. How I could be a hero to that female, who believed I could never save her in the end.

Maybe, I'm the fool.